January

K.C. KELLEY • BOB OSTROM

The
Child's
World

Published by The Child's World®
1980 Lookout Drive • Mankato, MN 56003-1705
800-599-READ • www.childsworld.com

Acknowledgments
The Child's World®: Mary Berendes, Publishing Director
The Design Lab: Design
Jody Jensen Shaffer: Editing and Fact-Checking

Photo credits
© Carrienelson1/Dreamstime.com:23 (bottom); Charles Brutlag/
Shutterstock.com: 13 (top); Elias Goldensky/Wikimedia Commons:
20 (top); fivepointsix/Shutterstock.com: 19 (bottom); Foodio/
Shutterstock.com: 11 (bottom); GeorgiosArt /iStock.com: 22
(bottom); Georgios Kollidas/Shutterstock.com: 22 (top); IZO/
Shutterstock.com: cover, 1, 5; HixnHix/Shutterstock.com: 13
(bottom); Kameleon007/iStock.com: 19 (bottom); Nikolenko
Roman/Shutterstock.com: 6; Olga Popova/Shutterstock.com: 20
(bottom); Petr Toman/Shutterstock.com: 12 (top); Photowitch/
Dreamstime.com: 19 (top); Rena Schild/Shutterstock.com: 11 (top);
Sborisov/Dreamstime.com: 18; scibak /iStock.com: 17; Wrangel/
Dreamstime.com: 23 (top); XiXinXing/Shutterstock.com: 10;
Zigzag Mountain Art/Shutterstock.com: 12 (bottom)

ISBN 9781626873667
LCCN 2014930705

Printed in the United States of America
Mankato, MN
July, 2014
PA02214

ABOUT THE AUTHOR

K.C. Kelley has written dozens of books for young readers on everything from sports to nature to history. He was born in January, loves April because that's when baseball begins, and loves to take vacations in August!

ABOUT THE ILLUSTRATOR

Bob Ostrom has been illustrating books for twenty years. A graduate of the New England School of Art & Design at Suffolk University, Bob has worked for such companies as Disney, Nickelodeon, and Cartoon Network. He lives in North Carolina with his wife and three children.

Contents

WELCOME TO JANUARY!

Happy New Year! Every year starts with January. It's time for us all to start another trip around the sun. That's what a year is—Earth does a full trip around the sun in 365 days. January 1 is the first of those days! January is a time to start new projects. New Year's Day is a holiday in most countries, too.

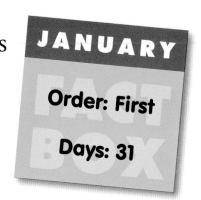

JANUARY

FACT BOX

Order: First

Days: 31

NOW THAT'S SLOW!

Have you heard the phrase "slow as molasses in January"? January is usually a very cold month. Molasses is a thick syrup. In cold weather, it's even thicker! It won't pour quickly then. So people sometimes say that something is moving as slow as molasses in a cold month!

HOW DID JANUARY GET ITS NAME?

The ancient Romans had gods for many parts of their lives. The god of beginnings and endings was called *Janus*. He was also the god of doorways. Janus had two faces. One looked ahead, and one looked behind. The first month was named for him, since he looked back at the old year and ahead to the new one.

Birthstone

Each month has a stone linked to it. People who have birthdays in that month call it their birthstone. For January, it's the garnet.

JANUARY AROUND THE WORLD

Here is the name of this month in other languages.

Chinese	Yī yuè
Dutch	Januari
English	January
French	Janvier
German	der Januar
Italian	Gennaio
Japanese	Ichigatsu
Spanish	Enero
Swahili	Januari

'ROUND AND 'ROUND WE GO

In one year, Earth takes 365 days to go around the sun. Other planets take more or less time. The planets closer to the sun take less time. The planets farther from the sun take more. One year on Jupiter, for example, takes 11.9 of our years on Earth. Our path around the sun is called an **orbit**.

BIG JANUARY HOLIDAYS

New Year's Day, January 1

Put on your party hats and sing! New Year's Day is the first day of the year... and the first holiday of the year. New Year's Day begins at midnight. Many people gather with their families for a day of feasting and football.

THE NEW PREZ!

Every four years, a new U.S. president is sworn in on January 20. On this January day, the new president takes office. This is called **inauguration** (in-awg-yu-RAY-shun). The new president promises to obey the Constitution and lead the people.

Dr. Martin Luther King, Jr. Day, Third Monday

Dr. King led people to call for equal rights in the 1960s. He said that people should protest injustice, but always peacefully. He inspired millions with his words. Sadly, Dr. King was killed in 1968. In his honor, King's birthday is now a national holiday. We remember his life and try to keep doing the work to make all people equal.

FOOTBALL FEVER!

The biggest college football games are called "bowl games." For a long time, the most important bowl games were played on New Year's Day. Fans would plan a whole day of watching great plays and big games. Now, some games remain on New Year's Day, but the national championship is played later in the month.

FUN JANUARY DAYS

January has more ways to celebrate than just making snow forts on New Year's Day! Here are some of the unusual holidays you can enjoy in January:

JANUARY 8

National Bubble Bath Day

JANUARY 14

Dress Up Your Pet Day

JANUARY 17

Kid Inventors' Day

JANUARY 19

National Popcorn Day

JANUARY 20

Penguin
Awareness Day

JANUARY 23

National Pie
Day

JANUARY 27

National Chocolate Cake Day

JANUARY 28

National Kazoo Day

JANUARY WEEKS AND MONTHS

Holidays don't just mean days…you can celebrate for a week, too! You can also have fun all month long. Find out more about these ways to enjoy January!

JANUARY WEEKS

Universal Letter-Writing Week: Your parents might remember what letters are! Before email and texting took over the world, people used pens and paper to write to each other. This week asks people to try the old-fashioned way again!

International Snowmobile Safety Week: Snowmobile fans love to ride fast through deep snow! These action machines thrill thousands of people. This week, the people who make the machines remind riders to be safe in the snow!

JANUARY MONTHS

National Blood Donor Month: A blood donor is a person who gives his or her blood. That blood can then be given to help other people.

National Oatmeal Month: What's better when it's chilly outside than a bowl of warm oatmeal? How about two bowls of warm oatmeal!

National Hobby Month: In the cold of January, many people spend time indoors working on their hobbies. Do you have a hobby?

National Braille and Literacy Month: Braille (BRAYL) is a type of writing that uses raised dots. It lets blind people read books, magazines, and more. The man who invented this writing, Louis Braille, was born in January.

National Polka Month: Grab your accordion and swing! Polka is a lively dance music from Eastern Europe. Play a few polka songs in honor of this musical month!

JANUARY AROUND THE WORLD

Countries around the world celebrate in January. Find these countries on the map. Then read about how people there have fun in January!

JANUARY 21

Errol Barrow Day, Barbados

The Caribbean island of Barbados used to be a British **colony**. In 1966, it became independent. This holiday honors the man who led the move toward freedom.

INDEPENDENCE DAYS

Many countries made New Year's Day the official beginning of their independence. America celebrates on July 4, but Haiti and Sudan also salute themselves on January 1. The country of Myanmar waits until January 4!

SECOND MONDAY

Coming of Age Day, Japan
In Japan, a person who turns 20 becomes an adult. This day honors those people and helps them get ready for adult life.

JANUARY 26

Australia Day, Australia
Until 1788, the only people who lived in Australia were native people called *Aborigines* (ab-uh-RIJ-uh-neez). On January 26 that year, British ships arrived carrying more than 1,000 people. Australia became a colony of Great Britain, but today it is independent. Australians celebrate Australia Day as the day people first came to that land. They also look back at how the new country hurt its original people.

JANUARY IN HISTORY

January 1, 1863

President Abraham Lincoln issued the Emancipation Proclamation. This document freed all people who were being held as slaves in the United States.

GOLD RUSH BEGINS

On January 24, 1848, a man named James Marshall made an amazing discovery. In a creek in northern California, he found gold! Marshall's find kicked off the California Gold Rush. Thousands of people seeking treasure poured into the area from around the world. Just over a year later, enough people had come that California became a state. Its nickname? The Golden State.

January 6, 1838

Samuel Morse demonstrated his new invention for communicating—the telegraph. Electric signals sent dots and dashes over wires. The dots and dashes—known as Morse Code—stood for letters.

January 15, 1967

The first Super Bowl was played in Los Angeles. The Green Bay Packers beat the Kansas City Chiefs, 35–10.

January 20, 1945

Franklin Delano Roosevelt was inaugurated for a fourth term as President of the United States. No one else ever served (or will ever serve) that many terms.

January 23, 1849

Elizabeth Blackwell becomes the first woman doctor in the United States. Today, about a third of all American doctors are women.

NEW STATES!

Seven states first joined the United States in January. Do you live in any of these? If you do, then make sure and say, "Happy Birthday!" to your state.

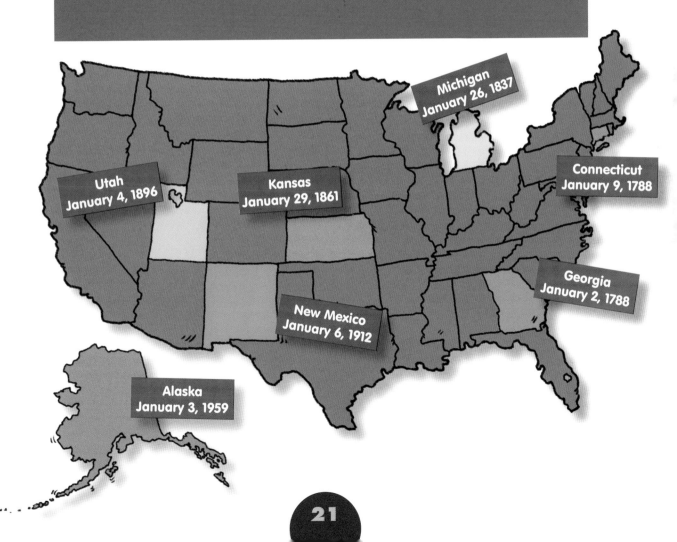

Michigan
January 26, 1837

Connecticut
January 9, 1788

Utah
January 4, 1896

Kansas
January 29, 1861

Georgia
January 2, 1788

New Mexico
January 6, 1912

Alaska
January 3, 1959

FAMOUS JANUARY BIRTHDAYS

January 4

Sir Isaac Newton

Newton first described many of the most important laws of physics, which is a part of science about the natural world. One famous story says that he "discovered" gravity when an apple fell on his head!

January 17

Benjamin Franklin

An inventor, writer, and leader of the American Revolution, Franklin was an amazing person. He was born in Boston in 1706 and lived until he was 84.

January 27

Wolfgang Amadeus Mozart
One of the greatest writers of classical music, Mozart was playing piano in public when he was only 6! He was born in Austria in 1756 and wrote hundreds of famous pieces of music.

January 29

Oprah Winfrey
One of the world's most famous women, she's a star on TV, in the movies, and even has her own magazine!

January 31

Jackie Robinson
The first African-American in Major League Baseball was born in Georgia. He was a star in all sports, but became a legend in one.

GLOSSARY

blood donor (BLUD DOH-nur) A blood donor is someone who gives his or her blood to help others.

braille (BRAYL) Braille is writing made up of raised dots. It allows blind people to read.

colony (KOL-uh-nee) A colony is an area of land that is ruled by another country.

inauguration (in-awg-yu-RAY-shun) An inauguration is a ceremony where a person, such as a president, officially begins his or her job.

orbit (OR-bit) An orbit is the path a planet takes around the sun.

INDEX